EARTH'S ROCKY PAST

MINERALS

Richard Spilsbury

PowerKiDS
press™

New York

Published in 2016 by **The Rosen Publishing Group**
29 East 21st Street, New York, NY 10010

Produced for Rosen by Calcium

Editors for Calcium: Sarah Eason and Harriet McGregor
Designers: Paul Myerscough and Jessica Moon
Illustrator: Venetia Dean

Picture credits: Cover: Shutterstock: Farbled; Inside: Dreamstime: Adeliepenguin 4–5b, Steve
Allen 26–27, Andreiorlov 24–25, Antoinettew 5r, Valentin Armianu 16–17t, Jeffrey Banke 19b,
Marcel Clemens 15t, Czalewski 9br, Fireflyphoto 6–7t, Amy Harris 8–9, Miroslava Holasová
14, Howardliuphoto 7r, Ikonoklastfotografie 21b, Zdenek Klucka 6b, Yury Kosourov 1, 16b,
Konstantin Lobastov 20, Laurentiu Lordache 18–19, Mopic 10, Mvogel 13r, Huguette Roe 26,
Teprzem 4t, Theroff97 27r, Wellford Tiller 21t, Ukrphoto 15b, Verdelho 25r; Shutterstock: Paulo
Afonso 11, Anyaivanova 22, MDD 12–13, Yulia Vybornyh 23; Wikimedia Commons: Monusco
Photos 17b.

Cataloging-in-Publication Data
Spilsbury, Richard.
Minerals / by Richard Spilsbury.
p. cm. — (Earth's rocky past)
Includes index.
ISBN 978-1-4994-0821-8 (pbk.)
ISBN 978-1-4994-0820-1 (6 pack)
ISBN 978-1-4994-0819-5 (library binding)
1. Minerals — Juvenile literature. I. Spilsbury, Richard, 1963-. II. Title.
QE365.2 S65 2016
549—d23

Manufactured in the United States of America
CPSIA Compliance Information: Batch WS15PK: For Further Information contact Rosen Publishing, New York, New York at 1-800-237-9932

CONTENTS

MINERALS

Minerals are solid substances that make up rocks. They are found in all rocks, from the tiny grains of sand on the shore to the high mountains that tower above the land. Minerals and rocks are used to make many of the things we need and use every day, from computers to buildings.

Minerals in the form of rocks are very useful to us. This rock is coal that is being cut into pieces to burn.

DEAD OR ALIVE?

Minerals are natural substances, formed by nature. They are not made by humans. Almost all of the substances we call minerals are **inorganic**. That means they have never been alive and are not formed from the remains or parts of plants or animals.

Mighty mountains such as the dramatic peaks of Patagonia, Chile, are made out of rocks. The rocks are made out of minerals!

ROCK STAR STORIES

Many minerals form beautiful and interesting **crystals**, but the most valuable of all are gemstones. There are more than 200 gemstones. The most precious are diamonds, rubies, sapphires, and emeralds. In their natural state, these gems do not look special, but when they are cut and polished they sparkle and shine.

Gemstone crystals are hard and tough enough to resist scratching and have beautiful, pure colors.

ELEMENTS EVERYWHERE

Minerals are made from **elements** found in Earth. Elements are simple substances that cannot be broken down into any other substance. Some minerals, like copper, contain only one element: copper. Most minerals are made of several elements. Quartz is a mineral made up of two elements: silicon and oxygen. Minerals are usually found in shapeless lumps or as special shapes we recognize as crystals. Crystals are solid structures with flat sides and sharp edges.

5

ROCK MINERALS

Minerals give rocks their different features, colors, and forms. The mineral crystals in most rocks are small and mixed together randomly. However, sometimes crystals of single minerals, like gold, form in the spaces in the rocks.

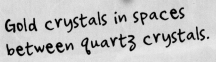

Gold crystals in spaces between quartz crystals.

GRANITE AND LIMESTONE

Sometimes when you look at a rock, you can see the different minerals from which it is formed. Granite contains three minerals: large crystals of a pink mineral called feldspar, a white mineral called quartz, and a dark mineral called mica. You can usually see all three colors in a lump of granite. Limestone is mostly made from calcite. The calclite mineral is usually white and makes limestone rock pale in color. Limestone blocks were the main building material used in many of the pyramids in ancient Egypt.

Close-up, you can see that granite is made from many different mineral crystals.

ROCK STAR STORIES

Around 30 percent of all minerals are silicates, making them Earth's most common type of mineral. Silicates include rocks like quartz and clay, which consist of silicon and oxygen (a gas in the air). More than 90 percent of the **mass** of the **Earth's crust** is made up of silicates.

Clues to the Past

Rocks used in pyramids give **archaeologists** a lot of clues about ancient Egypt. The limestone pyramids often had pink granite pillars and roof blocks. The limestone that the Egyptian builders used was dragged from nearby. The granite was brought from far away. As granite is very heavy, it must have been brought by ship up the Nile River and required many workers to move it.

limestone sphinx and pyramid

MAKING MINERALS

Most of the minerals in the rocks that make up Earth's crust come from deep beneath the ground. The crust we live on is cool, but the core (center) of our planet is incredibly hot. The hot layer of rocks below the crust is called the **mantle**. Here, rocks are so hot that they are molten and are called magma.

rock formed when lava cooled

RISING UP

Magma moves up through Earth's crust to the surface. As magma rises, it cools and moves farther from the hot core. As it cools, minerals in the magma become solid and form crystals. In some places, magma bursts suddenly out of the Earth when a volcano erupts. Outside the volcano, magma is called lava. As lava cools, the minerals inside it harden and form **igneous rock**.

Pumice is a type of igneous rock that forms when lava cools slowly. It is mainly composed of silicate minerals. If pumice is found at a particular location it is evidence that there was a volcano in that region in the past. The age of the pumice tells scientists roughly when the eruption happened.

ROCK STAR STORIES

Geodes are hollow rocks that contain crystals. Some geodes start out as air bubbles inside lava. When rainwater lands on the hard rock around the air bubble, the water **dissolves** parts of the rock and flows through to the air bubble. Over millions of years, minerals dissolved in the water gradually form crystals on the inside of the hollow rock.

Cracking open a geode to find the crystals hidden inside is very exciting!

SPACE AND WATER

Some minerals come from space or from deep underwater! **Meteorites** are rocks that fly through space and crash into Earth. They bring minerals to Earth. Other minerals form when water seeps into the Earth's crust.

METEORITE COLLISION

Meteorites formed in space at the same time as Earth and the other planets. When meteorites hit Earth they break up and the minerals that formed them became part of Earth's crust. Kamacite, which contains the element iron, is one of the minerals that arrived on Earth in meteorites.

When rocks glow on their approach to Earth it is called a meteor shower.

HOT WATER

As water enters cracks in Earth's crust, it is heated up by the hot mantle rock. The water dissolves some of the mantle and mixes with mantle elements. This **solution** forms new minerals when it cools. Some solutions burst out of holes in the ground as geysers. They form mineral walls around the holes as the water **evaporates**.

Clues to the Past

Scientists use minerals from meteorites to estimate the age of planet Earth. Meteorites and Earth formed at the same time but the rocks in Earth's crust are constantly being created, changed, and destroyed as part of the rock cycle (see pages 12-13). Most iron meteorites stay the same, so by learning how old they are, scientists can discover Earth's age too: more than 4.5 billion years!

ROCK STAR STORIES

When meteorite rocks are polished they reveal beautiful patterns of lines called Widmanstatten patterns. The lines are named after the man who discovered them in 1808. These patterns are formed from crisscrossing lines of crystals that developed as the meteorite slowly cooled.

crisscross mineral patterns in an iron meteorite

RECYCLED MINERALS

Minerals form many different kinds of rocks but they can be divided into three main groups: igneous, **sedimentary**, and **metamorphic**. The rock cycle is the process in which these three types of rock change form. In this way the minerals within the rocks are **recycled** over very long periods of time.

THE ROCK CYCLE

Igneous rocks form when the minerals that make up magma cool and harden. Particles on the surface of igneous rocks are **weathered** by rain, ice, and wind. Water and wind then **erode** these pieces of sediment somewhere new. The sediments pile up and press together to form sedimentary rock. Heat and pressure underground can rearrange elements in sedimentary rocks to form new minerals and new rocks, called metamorphic rock.

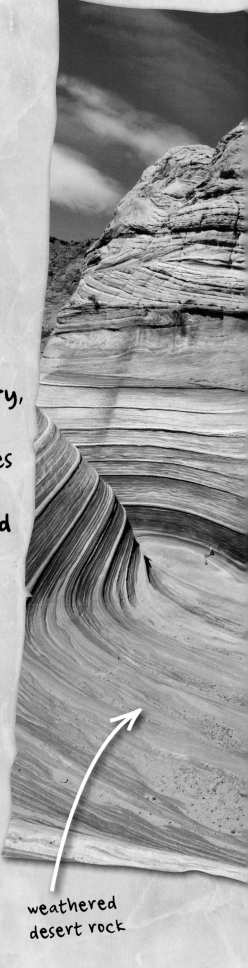

weathered desert rock

Sedimentary rocks often contain fossils. When sea animals die and sink to the ocean floor, water carrying tiny pieces of sediment gradually soaks into their empty shells. Over time, minerals from the water replace the minerals that make up the shell. These minerals turn into rock that is exactly the same shape as the shell, creating a fossil.

ROCK STAR STORIES

Marble is a metamorphic rock formed from limestone, a sedimentary rock. When the limestone changes, its minerals form interlocking crystals in the marble. The 1922 Lincoln Memorial in Washington, DC, is a famous marble monument. Designer Henry Bacon insisted on using white Georgia marble for the statue, Tennessee pink marble for the floor, and Alabama marble for the ceiling. Using rock from across the United States symbolized how Lincoln united the country.

marble statue of the Lincoln Memorial

TYPES OF MINERALS

fluorite crystal

There are more than 3,000 different types of minerals, and more are being discovered all the time. Some minerals look similar, so **geologists** have figured out different ways to identify them all. They can be divided into **metals** and nonmetals, and identified by their hardness, color, and how shiny they are.

COLOR IDENTIFICATION

Some minerals can be identified by their color. Azurite is always deep blue. Others, like fluorite, come in several different colors. Fluorite must be identified by other features, like its hardness and the way in which it breaks. When split, fluorite often breaks into pieces that are the shape of an **octahedron**.

RECOGNIZING SHINE

Some minerals are identified by their **luster**, or shininess. Quartz and the metal form of mineral gold both reflect light better than other minerals so appear to shine. Some minerals come in a range of colors but can be identified because they always look the same color when ground to a powder. For example, the mineral calcite comes in many different colors and shapes, but when crushed it is always white.

ROCK STAR STORIES

iron pyrite

Iron pyrite is called "fool's gold" because this mineral has a similar luster and color to gold. In fact, they look so similar that some people have been fooled into thinking this cheap and common mineral is really gold!

Clues to the Past

Malachite is an unusual and beautiful mineral containing light and dark green bands of color. Malachite tells us that the metal mineral copper was in the area in the past, and might still be found nearby today. This is because malachite forms after hot water dissolves copper from underground rock.

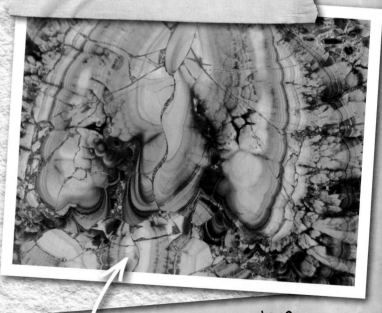

Malachite is used as a gemstone because of the color and patterns that identify it.

AROUND THE WORLD

Some minerals are very common. Quartz is found in desert sand and on seashores all over the world. Other minerals, like gold, are rare and only found in certain places.

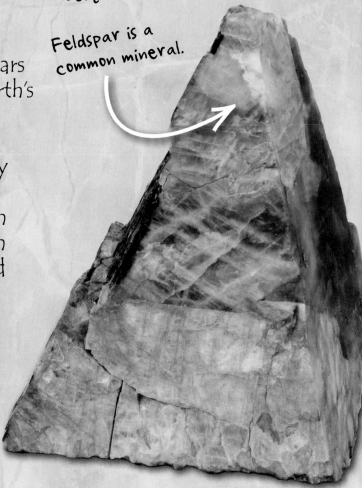

Sahara Desert

PLENTIFUL OR RARE

Minerals like quartz and feldspars make up more than half of Earth's crust. They are easily found and exist in large quantities in a lot of places. That is why they are not valued as much as rare minerals that are only found in specific places. Gold is found in small amounts in rocks around the world, but there are larger amounts in certain countries, like South Africa. Red beryl is a very rare mineral. So far it has only been found in parts of Utah and New Mexico.

Feldspar is a common mineral.

Clues to the Past

Diamonds brought to the Earth's surface in volcanic eruptions have a mineral trapped inside them that reveals some of Earth's secrets. The diamonds contain bright blue ringwoodite, which only forms at 250 to 400 miles (400 to 640 km) beneath Earth's surface and has water trapped within it. Scientists believe there may be several times the amount of water inside our planet than in the oceans!

ROCK STAR STORIES

Coltan is a black, tar-like mineral that is very good at holding and moving electrical signals. That is why it is used in cell phones, computers, and a wide range of other electronic devices. It is quite rare and only found in a small number of places. Almost half of the coltan used around the world comes from Central Africa.

coltan mine in Central Africa

MINING MINERALS

Iron ore is heated with other minerals to make steel.

Mining is the removal of minerals and metals from the Earth. Mining minerals can be expensive so before work begins, companies hire a geologist to figure out whether there are high quality minerals or metals in a location.

INVESTIGATING THE GROUND

Geologists drill holes and collect material from inside Earth. They study it to figure out how much of the minerals or metals are in that location and whether there is enough to make it worth mining there.

TYPES OF MINES

Mining for minerals is done in many different ways. Minerals found near Earth's surface can be extracted using an open pit mining method. This is when workers dig a pit in Earth's surface. Other minerals are hidden deep inside Earth. They are removed by digging a deep shaft, or tunnel, straight down into the ground. Minerals that are removed from the Earth are called **ores**.

ROCK STAR STORIES

Bauxite ore is the world's main source of aluminum, which we use to make cans, foil, and many other items. Bauxite is found a few feet underground, so is usually mined using the open pit method.

Clues to the Past

In the past people panned for gold. They washed gravel in a pan to separate out pieces of gold. The gold grains they found told them whether a bigger source of gold was nearby. Rough grains with hard edges suggest that a source of gold is nearby. Grains become smooth when they are eroded over long distances, so the smoother the grains of gold, the farther away the source.

panned gold grains

USEFUL MINERALS

People use minerals every day and in many different ways. Minerals provide the buildings we live in, the magazines we read, and the cell phones we rely on. The world would simply not be the same without minerals!

MATERIALS FOR LIFE

Rocks cut straight from the land make our buildings. Slate is sliced into pieces to make roof tiles and granite slabs are used for countertops. Some minerals are crushed and mixed with other substances to make building materials. For example, clay minerals are used to make bricks and floor tiles. Quartz from sand is used to make glass, and kaolinite is used to make paper, mugs, and toilets.

Stained glass is made by processing quartz.

Minerals are hard and solid and can last a long time in rock form. We have evidence of how people used minerals in the past. Flint is a type of quartz that is colored by the other minerals found in it. It can be cut to give a very sharp edge. Tools and weapons made from flint have been found that date from **prehistoric** times. The types of tools made and how well-used they are tells us much about how people lived in the past.

flint arrowhead

ROCK STAR STORIES

When a tooth is damaged it can be covered with a thin layer of porcelain, like a false fingernail fits over a nail. Porcelain is made by mixing clay minerals with other substances and heating it until it becomes glasslike.

making porcelain caps for teeth

LIVING MINERALS

Minerals not only make up the rocks of our planet, they are also needed by living things. When rocks are broken down in the rock cycle, the minerals become part of the soil. Plants take in minerals from soil through their roots. Animals take in minerals when they eat plants or plant-eating animals.

MINERALS FOR PLANTS

Plants need a group of minerals called phosphates, which help the plants grow. That is one reason why plants grow well on soil near volcanoes, where minerals blasted from the volcano have become part of the soil. Farmers can also add **fertilizers**, which contain minerals, to soil to help plants grow.

grape vines growing on dark volcanic soil

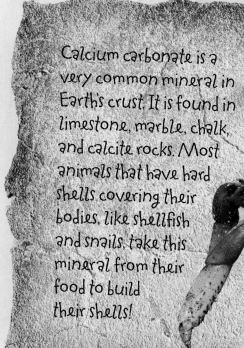

Calcium carbonate is a very common mineral in Earth's crust. It is found in limestone, marble, chalk, and calcite rocks. Most animals that have hard shells covering their bodies, like shellfish and snails, take this mineral from their food to build their shells!

Crabs are armored with a shell containing calcium carbonate.

MINERALS FOR ANIMALS

When animals, including humans, eat plants, or plant-eating animals, they get minerals from that food. For example, beef contains the mineral iron, which is important for making healthy blood, and milk contains calcium, which helps build healthy bones and teeth.

Clues to the Past

The discovery of Roman salt factories gives us an insight to the importance of salt in Roman times. The factories removed the mineral halite (salt) from water. The salt was then used as money and soldiers were even paid in salt. The English word salary comes from the Latin word for salt: sal. Today, we eat salt, but it is important not to have too much salt in our diets.

MIGHTY METALS

Metals are very useful minerals. They allow us to make all sorts of things, from airplanes, ships, and buildings, to cans and jewelry.

USEFUL PROPERTIES

Each metal has its own particular properties. Some metals are extremely hard and some can be bent and shaped much more easily. Aluminum is used to make cans because it is light and easy to shape. Steel is very strong, light, and can be shaped easily, so is used for sinks and saucepans, ships and building frames.

COPPER AND JEWELS

Electricity moves easily through copper, which makes copper metal perfect for use in electrical wires. Engineers have been using copper in electronics for years. Precious metals, like gold, are expensive and used mainly for jewelry and expensive watches.

Roller coaster tracks twist and dip to give an exciting ride. They are built from incredibly strong steel.

ROCK STAR STORIES

Gold is used in space. Many satellites have thin sheets of gold to protect them from the sun's heat. Satellites are machines in space that take pictures to help people make weather forecasts or send television, radio, and other signals around the planet. Astronauts have a thin layer of gold on the front of their helmet visors to protect them from the sun's glare. The James Webb Space Telescope has an incredibly thin coating of gold on its mirrors to reflect light to help us see galaxies far, far away!

Clues to the Past

Copper weapons have been found dating from between 7,000 and 10,000 years ago. These discoveries are important. They show us when humans started to make things from metal instead of stone. We can learn much about how people lived from the types of tools, ornaments, and weapons they made. Copper was one of the first metals used because it can be found in rocks as a pure element.

copper wire

MINERALS MATTER

Minerals take millions of years to form so when we remove them from the ground and use them, they cannot easily be replaced. Some of the devices we use also require rare minerals to work, and these are even harder to replace. Mines destroy habitats where plants and animals live and can pollute the land and water around them.

SOURCING A SOLUTION

Recycling is one way of reducing the amount of minerals the world uses. To recycle an object, it is broken up and the minerals in it are used to make new products. For example, the steel in cars can be recycled and used to make new cars. Aluminum cans are melted and reshaped into new cans. Computers and other electronic devices are recycled so that the metals inside them, including copper and gold, can be used again. Minerals matter, so think about how much you use and how much you can recycle too!

Cars can be recycled into metal for new cars.

aluminum cans

ROCK STAR STORIES

The aluminum drink can is the most recycled drink container on Earth. It is possible to recycle aluminum over and over again. Used aluminum cans can be recycled and back on a store's shelves as new drink cans in as little as two months!

Clues to the Past

Identifying and understanding rocks and minerals here on Earth and discovering how they formed helps us learn about the past on Mars! A type of mineral called phyllosilicates has been found on Mars. This mineral is a little like clay and forms in wet places here on Earth. If phyllosilicates also exist on Mars, that means there must have been water on the planet in the past.

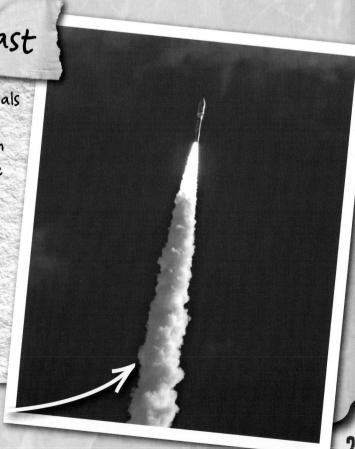

Missions to Mars have discovered minerals like those on Earth.

ROCK YOUR WORLD!

Collecting mineral samples is a fun thing to do and a great way to learn about the shapes, colors, and forms of the world's amazing minerals. Here are some ideas to get you started.

DO YOUR RESEARCH

Before you begin collecting minerals, learn more about them by reading online. Buy or loan from the library a mineral identification book with pictures. You may also be able to see mineral collections in a local museum.

FINDING MINERALS

You can buy mineral samples from shops and websites, but you can also look for minerals on beaches, hills, parks, and backyards. When you go looking for minerals, remember the following:

- Go with an adult or tell them where you are going. Check that where you are mineral hunting is safe.
- Wear tough boots in case you stand on sharp rocks or a rock rolls toward your feet.
- Wear gloves when picking through rocks and soil as they can contain bacteria that could make you sick.
- Take a bag with you for collecting samples.

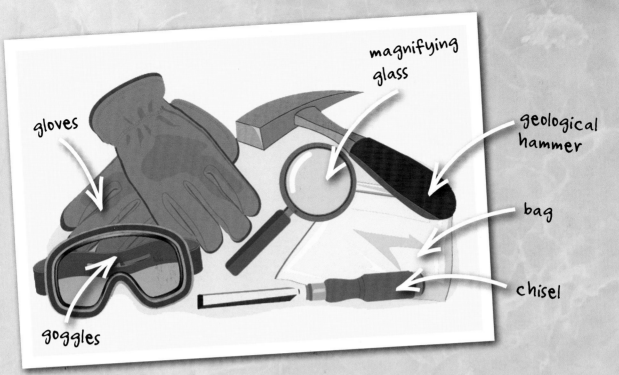

gloves

magnifying glass

geological hammer

bag

chisel

goggles

- Other tools you may need include a geological hammer to break rocks, goggles to protect your eyes from flying rock particles, a hand lens or magnifying glass for looking closely at rock samples, and a chisel for chopping off interesting rock fragments.

DISPLAY YOUR RESULTS

When you have a mineral collection, you will need to think about how to display and sort your findings. Some collectors group their mineral collections by type, color, or size. You could label them, and display them so you can show other people your collection, too!

TRY IT OUT!

Try gemstone panning to find minerals to add to your collection. There are many locations where you can practice your panning technique on bags of mixed mining rock. After washing away the waste and bits of unwanted rock, each bag may contains many different minerals.

GLOSSARY

archaeologists People who study objects from human history.

crystals Solid substances that are naturally symmetrical and regular in form.

dissolves When a liquid appears to break down a solid. The solid seems to disappear into the liquid.

Earth's crust Outer layer of hard rock that forms Earth's surface.

elements Substances made entirely from one type of atom, like oxygen, hydrogen, or iron.

erode When pieces of rocks are carried somewhere new.

evaporates When a liquid changes to a gas.

fertilizers Substances farmers put on fields to help plants grow.

geologists People who study what the Earth is made of and how it formed.

habitats Places where plants and animals live.

igneous rock Rock formed from magma.

inorganic Something that is not and has never been alive.

luster Brightness or shine.

mantle Very deep layer of hot rock beneath Earth's crust.

mass A measure of how much matter (stuff) is in an object.

metals Substances like gold or copper that usually look shiny, can be melted, through which electricity and heat move easily, and can usually be shaped.

metamorphic Rock changed from its original form by heat and/or pressure.

meteorites Rocks from space.

octahedron A flat-sided solid object with eight sides.

ores Rocks in Earth's crust that contain valuable minerals.

pollute To add dirty or harmful substances to air, soil, or water.

prehistoric Before written history.

recycled Changed into something new.

sedimentary Rocks formed when tiny pieces of rock or shells are squashed and heated in layers.

solution A liquid in which a substance is dissolved.

weathered To be worn away by wind, water, and ice.

FURTHER READING

BOOKS

Fretland VanVoorst, Jenny. *Gems* (Rocks and Minerals). Edina, MN: Core Library, 2014.

Green, Dan. *Rocks and Minerals* (Discover More). New York, NY: Scholastic, 2013.

Hirsch, Rebecca E. *Crystals* (Rocks and Minerals). Edina, MN: Core Library, 2014.

Tomecek, Steve. *Dirtmeister's Nitty Gritty Planet Earth: All About Rocks, Minerals, Fossils, Earthquakes, Volcanoes, & Even Dirt!*. Washington, DC: National Geographic Children's Books, 2015.

WEBSITES

Due to the changing nature of Internet links, PowerKids Press has developed an online list of websites related to the subject of this book. This site is updated regularly. Please use this link to access the list: www.powerkidslinks.com/erp/mineral

INDEX